THE
ARIES
ORACLE

THE
ARIES
ORACLE

INSTANT ANSWERS FROM
YOUR COSMIC SELF

STELLA FONTAINE

greenfinch

Introduction

Welcome to your zodiac oracle,
carefully crafted especially for you
Aries, and brimming with the wisdom
of the universe.

**Is there a tricky-to-answer question niggling at you
and you need an answer?**

Whenever you're unsure whether to say 'yes' or 'no',
whether to go back or to carry on, whether to trust
or to turn away, make some time for a personal
session with your very own oracle. Drawing on your
astrological profile, your zodiac oracle will guide
you in understanding, interpreting and answering
those burning questions that life throws your way.
Discovering your true path will become an
enlightening journey of self-actualization.

Humans have long cast their eyes heavenwards to seek answers from the universe. For millennia the sun, moon and stars have been our constant companions as they repeat their paths and patterns across the skies. We continue to turn to the cosmos for guidance, trusting in the deep and abiding wisdom of the universe as we strive for fulfilment, truth and understanding.

The most basic and familiar aspect of astrology draws on the twelve signs of the zodiac, each connected to a unique constellation as well as its own particular colours, numbers and characteristics. These twelve familiar signs are also known as the sun signs: Aries, Taurus, Gemini, Cancer, Leo, Virgo, Libra, Scorpio, Sagittarius, Capricorn, Aquarius and Pisces.

Aries Taurus Gemini Cancer Leo Virgo

Libra Scorpio Sagittarius Capricorn Aquarius Pisces

Each sign is associated with an element (fire, air, earth or water), and also carries a particular quality: cardinal (action-takers), fixed (steady and constant) and mutable (changeable and transformational). Beginning to understand these complex combinations, and to recognize the layered influences they bring to bear on your life, will unlock your own potential for personal insight, self-awareness and discovery.

In our data-flooded lives, now more than ever it can be difficult to know where to turn for guidance and advice. With your astrology oracle always by your side, navigating life's twists and turns will become a smoother, more mindful process. Harness the prescience of the stars and tune in to the resonance of your sun sign with this wisdom-packed guide that will lead you to greater self-knowledge and deeper confidence in the decisions you are making. Of course, not all questions are created equal; your unique character, your circumstances and the issues with which you find yourself confronted all add up to a conundrum unlike any other... but with your question in mind and your zodiac oracle in your hand, you're already halfway to the answer.

Aries:
MARCH 21 TO APRIL 19

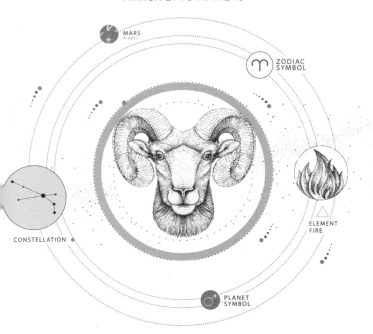

Element: Fire
Quality: Cardinal
Named for the constellation Aries (the ram)
Ruled by: Mars
Opposite: Libra
Characterized by: Confidence, passion, determination
Colour: Red

How to Use This Book

You can engage with your oracle whenever you need to but, for best results, create an atmosphere of calm and quiet, somewhere you will not be disturbed, making a place for yourself and your question to take priority. Whether this is a particular physical area you turn to in times of contemplation, or whether you need to fence off a dedicated space within yourself during your busy day, that all depends on you and your circumstances. Whichever you choose, it is essential that you actively put other thoughts and distractions to one side in order to concentrate upon the question you wish to answer.

Find a comfortable position, cradle this book lightly in your hands, close your eyes, centre yourself. Focus on the question you wish to ask. Set your intention gently and mindfully towards your desire to answer this question, to the exclusion of all other thoughts and mind-chatter. Allow all else to float softly away, as you remain quiet and still, gently watching the shape and form of the question you wish to address. Gently deepen and slow your breathing.

Tune in to the ancient resonance of your star sign, the vibrations of your surroundings, the beat of your heart and the flow of life and the universe moving in and around you. You are one with the universe.

Now simply press the book between your palms as you clearly and distinctly ask your question (whether aloud or in your head), then open it at any page. Open your eyes. Your advice will be revealed.

Read it carefully. Take your time turning this wisdom over in your mind, allowing your thoughts to surround it, to absorb it, flow with it, then to linger and settle where they will.

Remember, your oracle will not provide anything as blunt and brutal as a completely literal answer. That is not its role. Rather, you will be gently guided towards the truth you seek through your own consciousness, experience and understanding. And as a result, you will grow, learn and flourish.

Let's begin.

Close your eyes.

Hold the question you want
answered clearly in your mind.

Open your oracle to any page to
reveal your cosmic insight.

With Mars watching over you,
and that fire flowing through you,
you know that staying still for too long
is not an option for you Aries...
time to move.

Self-improvement is all well and good but be sure it improves the way you interact with the real world rather than just with yourself.

Usually you are so in charge, Aries, it can feel very disorienting when things seem not to be going your way. But, as ever, there is a greater plan at work here. Breathe, stay in the moment, try to let go of that you are seeking to hold and this too shall pass.

When you know what it is you really want, there is nothing more powerful than that hard-headed determination Aries is so famous for.

There is no point in play-acting having a good time if you are just not that into it Aries. Take some time out of the crowd to spend by yourself, follow your instincts.

Self-affirmation is a crucial part of owning your identity. Be open about your opinions and desires.

Even if your concentration
is not strong right now, you can
count on your courage and confidence
to guide you through. Aries, you can
cope with this.

Balance may be hard to achieve but finding it in your own life is essential.

A quiet favour might make everything easier for you at the moment Aries. Especially if you haven't previously had the smoothest relationship with this particular person, be sure to express your gratitude.

Life is too short for pettiness, holding grudges or one-upmanship Aries. Demonstrating your philosophy of 'just getting on with things' will signal to others that you expect the same of them.

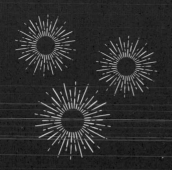

Relax and let things be; the essential spark will ignite again soon enough.

Creativity will be an enormous
help right now Aries; make the time
required to think this through properly
and allow inspiration to bubble up. Be
careful not to let your tendency to
rush ahead send you off course – this
demands a different approach.

Motivation and confidence
are big positives for you Aries.
Just don't let this one spark that
competitive streak you find so
difficult to keep in check.

Planning ahead doesn't always guarantee the results you think you want. It might feel like things aren't going your way, but you need to ask yourself whether it really matters? Keep that famous Aries fire burning and energy flowing, and soon enough you will be out the other side.

Sometimes compromise feels impossible to achieve. Bide your time and balance will be restored.

Try to reframe this challenge
as an opportunity for growth rather
than a trigger for your insecurity.
You are enough and you are
worth it.

Of course it doesn't come easily
to you, with your hard-headed ram
instincts, but try not to see this
as a competition.

Your energy is second to none Aries (congratulations, you win at energy!). But be careful you don't burn yourself out and try not to exhaust those around you while you're at it.

Your reputation for being friendly, warm and open is well deserved – you're great company. But try to remember to be true to yourself as well; being liked shouldn't be another of the competitions you feel so compelled to win.

Try giving something back
this time, rather than focusing on
what might be in this for you.

Look for adventure a little closer to home than usual Aries – don't overlook the familiar.

Time to showcase those talents of yours Aries – let your light shine.

Let go of that which no longer
serves you – thoughts, relationships,
situations, they all run the risk of
becoming stagnant. Take a
deep breath and release
it all on the exhale.

Whatever holding patterns you have found yourself in, now it's time to shake them off, brush yourself down and charge forwards again.

It will not be the easiest path, but this is the one you are destined to travel. Head down, one foot in front of the other and carry on.

Your bold, ambitious
approach can sometimes trap
you into too aggressive a pace.
Uncertain times call for decisive
action, but you must take care
as you choose your path.

New things will come into
your life, as long as you are prepared
to allow them.

Being of service to others
must be done with love and purity
of heart. If you are in it to win it, this
one is not going to go your way.
Success on this occasion might
look slightly different to what
you're used to. Time to rethink.

Moving out of your comfort zone will show you new ways to achieve the next level. Time to shake things up a little.

Ruled by Mars, it's no wonder situations often look like a battle to you Aries! But this time you would do better to cool that hot head of yours before making a decision.

Action and impulse are
such intrinsic parts of your Aries
approach, it can be difficult for you to
understand that coming first is not
always the most important thing. This
time, although it won't be easy, it's
important to step aside.

Gentler, more timid signs
might find your zest for life a little
overwhelming at times. But your
energy serves you well, and ultimately
those around you will benefit.

Think of yourself as the diamond (your birthstone) that couldn't exist without pressure and intense heat. Lower your horns and charge this challenge head-on, Aries; you know you've got what it takes.

Sparks will fly if you find yourself
butting heads with an immoveable
problem, because you are not one to
give up on pushing for what you want.
For everyone's sake, take a moment to
consider whether there might be
another way around this one.

It seems you already know
the answer, but it's the question that
you are afraid of.

Aries – skull and head and eyes
and brain-heat. Slow this one down,
relax and activate your gut instinct
to find the truth this time.

Sometimes, 'do nothing' is a valid action, impossible as it might seem to the charging ram. Wait for this one to wash over you, if you can bear to, and the results will be infinitely better.

Bold, direct and full of fire... sound like anyone you know? Make these traits work for you this time; the situation is crying out for a decisive response.

Whether you are seeing red with rage or blazing with passion, fire is your element. But remember to hold some back for when you really need it; you can spark something huge if you just bide your time.

Embrace the opportunity to
put yourself first; taking the initiative
is to be applauded.

A more comprehensive understanding will help simplify your approach. Don't allow yourself to be distracted from the task at hand. Time devoted to deepening your learning is never wasted.

Focus on expanding your
knowledge, whether through
reading, talking, exploring or simply
asking questions and listening.
Understanding is key.

Improved focus and patience
will result if you set aside your
ram-headed determination to win
for a while. Clarity and attention go
hand in hand on this one.

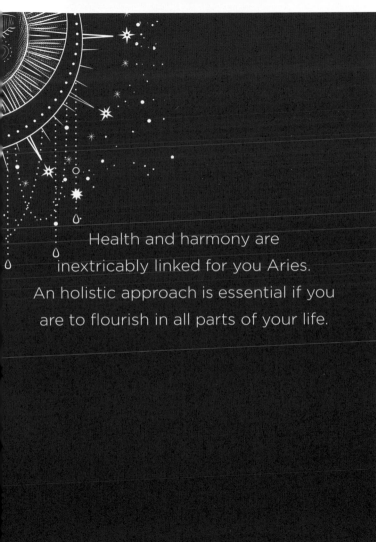

Health and harmony are
inextricably linked for you Aries.
An holistic approach is essential if you
are to flourish in all parts of your life.

Admired as one of the most singular and focused signs, now it's time to make the most of your Aries talents. Do not shy away from this challenge. Nothing worth doing seems easy at first.

Remain open to all possibilities for exploration and adventure; scratch the itch for new discoveries and fresh opportunities when it strikes.

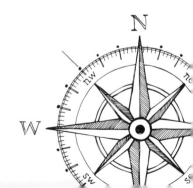

Your tendency towards opportunism has served you well in the past and you must allow yourself to explore any potential advantages that come your way – after all, now is your time.

On this occasion, a big-picture approach is the only way to achieve an outcome that works for everyone – music to your Aries ears. Relinquishing control might feel risky, but you need to rise above the detail and go with it. There may not be another way to secure that win.

Relax and allow things to be as they are. The small things do have a way of working themselves out, you know.

You are an interesting person
and so, inevitably, complicated. You
carry plenty of issues with you, but
also a wealth of talents. When an
opportunity arises to make the
most of your skills, take it.

You may not believe that you deserve this opportunity; set that worry to the side for the time being. Instead, focus fully on what you need to do to adapt and accept the lucky break which looks to be coming your way.

Gaining the confidence of others
is all you need to do right now to
clarify confusion about what has been
going on and to protect your
reputation. Make the effort, invest the
time and answer the questions.

Your first impulse was the right one, although initially it may have seemed to make little sense. Embrace your Aries-tendency to push ahead and get on with it.

Planning a journey or some other
kind of big adventure will feed
your immediate hunger for a bit of
excitement Aries. But ultimately, some
bigger changes are needed. Is this just
wanderlust, or something deeper and
more significant nagging at you?

Prepare to see the need for a change as a hiccup rather than an obstacle, potential excitement rather than a drag. How you frame this will make all the difference.

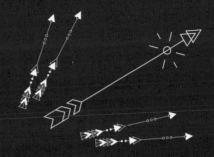

A little competition suits your style Aries, go ahead and enjoy the challenge! Just don't get so carried away that you charge ahead too aggressively, shoving everyone else aside to get to pole position.

Creating warm memories relies on building trust Aries. Allow yourself to align with others.

A gentle glow will light your
heart in the near future Aries. Far
from the fireworks and lightning you
think you crave, this one will be a
slow-burning, long-lasting warmth.

No one can deny it's easier
to stick to the safe questions, but is
this really the one you want an answer
to right now? Give it a little more
thought, be brave and ask again.

Others sometimes describe
your approach as 'headstrong' or
'stubborn' (the very idea!), when in
fact you know perfectly well that it is
pure commitment. Concern yourself
less with how other people see this
issue; be loyal to yourself.

Often you don't take enough time to simply be in the moment Aries, you're so busy charging forwards all the time. Celebrate how far you have come and what you have managed to achieve, rather than focusing on how much further there is to go.

Take a few moments today to quiet the ticking clock in your head and spend some time in nature – the answer will reveal itself. This is a tricky one, but not for the reasons you think.

As clever and ambitious as you are, sometimes you need to take a pause and look around while you wait for the world to catch up with you. There is something you still need to know.

Relishing the feeling of pride
in your achievements is vital to your
sense of living life well. Let pleasure
rule this moment.

You are a charge-ahead sign Aries, and that can make overly emotional or instinctual people and situations difficult for you to deal with. Try to remember that they likely struggle just as much to understand your motivations and actions. Take the time to explain yourself a little more clearly and to listen a little more intently.

Your Aries drive and ambition
might not have served you well on this
occasion – it is important to slow
down, revise your thinking and
perhaps even investigate further. The
details are not exactly as they might
have seemed at first.

Although it doesn't quite fit with your bold and ambitious head-first approach to life, this time you need to acknowledge that there are several possible routes and it is not at all clear which will be most effective.
Proceed with caution.

You may find it difficult to
relinquish control this time, especially
when you are so wedded to fast
outcomes and moving on quickly. But
learn to trust your stars; the path
ahead is already lit for you to follow.

Determination, motivation, cheerful unrelenting energy and leadership potential make you a sign to be reckoned with Aries. But you cannot fully control this situation on your own. Ask for help, and then allow it.

Change is on its way. It is not
time to turn a blind eye to the details,
much as you would love to. But make
best use of that relentless positivity
you are so known for and stay
open to possibilities.

Trust your intuition to spark a few connections for you; this one is more complicated than just what you can see on the surface.

Your impulse towards
self-determination is a powerful
and productive one Aries, and it brings
you many wins. But you must guard
against it tipping into a tendency
towards egotism and selfishness.

Your Aries impulsivity will not necessarily help you win this time. Consider the opinions of others – they might have actually taken the time to think this one through.

You are courageous and prone to fiery outbursts, but surely that's no surprise for a sign ruled by Mars, the bringer of war? Harness that energy to tackle this problem, but don't misdirect your anger or it could land you in all sorts of hot water.

You are fiercely loyal, highly energetic, fun to be around and the most brilliant company. But you will only be able to keep bringing your best-self if you allow time for your energy to replenish. Even *you* need downtime occasionally. You'll be ready to face the world again (and all those delicious challenges awaiting you) in no time.

With exciting new opportunities peeking around the corner, now is not the time to be overly cautious Aries. Don't hesitate to move forwards and grasp these longed-for chances with both hands.

Much as it goes against your impulsive nature, you need to play the long game and keep your powder dry. A sequence of small wins, rather than one huge explosive display of talent, will be the secret to your success.

With Libra as your opposite sign, sometimes you need to remember that balance and a measured approach can be more effective than leaping first and looking later.

Patience and persistence do not come naturally to you, but it might be worth learning how to weave these into your skills repertoire. These characteristics could hold the key to solving this one.

Your life's fullest potential will
not be achieved through the pursuit
of material things, but in nurturing and
acknowledging the value in those
around you.

Much as you hate to do it Aries, now might be time to revise your opinion about this one; there is a chance that you might not have it quite right. Unthinkable as it is, this does happen to you once in a while. It is time to at least consider the possibility that perhaps you might have been wrong.

Power struggles crop up all the time
for you; you can't bear being told what
to do or having to live by someone
else's rules. Take your time thinking
this one through and remember that
you don't have to charge straight
ahead into whatever you perceive the
problem to be. Find a way around,
rather than confronting this with your
ram-head lowered, ready for battle.

Direct and uncomplicated as you are Aries, it is important to remember that small details can be key in providing the structure and skeleton of things (even though all that pickiness often makes you want to turn tail and flee!). If you can't bear it, enlist the help of someone who can.

All relationships run into
difficult ground now and again;
spend some time thinking this through
so you can be absolutely clear what
it is you are dealing with before
you take any action.

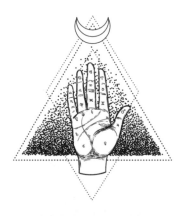

Of course, anything is possible, especially for a proactive, big-picture Aries. But you might need to look at this one a different way. The direction will make all the difference.

Perplexing as it may seem, your direct approach and penchant for unvarnished speech sometimes goes underappreciated. Lean into your intuition this time and keep your advice to yourself. This might not be the time for speaking your mind.

Conflict and slightly
bumpy relationship terrain are not
unfamiliar to you, but you are more
than capable of dealing with them. On
this occasion though you should resist
the temptation to wade in, sort it out
and package it neatly away in the
'wins' pile; just watch and wait.

Take all advice onboard and
be sure you pursue your own research
as well. Someone unexpected may
have a useful nugget of wisdom or
insight to offer. Then make a decision
and get on with it.

Add a little distance into
your relationships right now Aries,
you need some breathing space (for
everybody's sake) and time to clear
out all those emotions that have been
clouding your thinking for a while now.

Grab an opportunity for
some excitement Aries, even if it
means taking a risk.

Share your ideas with people
who will benefit from hearing them
Aries, rather than those who already
agree. Talking just because you enjoy
the sound of your own voice benefits
no-one, not even you.

Your perseverance will pay off soon, as suddenly things that not so long ago seemed confusing start to make sense. Possibility and purpose will become clear, and new ideas and creativity will bubble up for you.

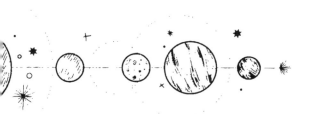

Think outside your usual way of doing things to consider a more philosophical approach. A willingness to compromise would be a very useful addition, too. Your heart, your head (and your stress levels) will thank you.

Such a powerful fire sign, you
know better than most the benefit
of allowing enough fuel and oxygen to
support the flame. Keep your feet
planted firmly on the ground
as you reach for the stars.

It's time to stoke the famous
Aries fire, to focus on nurturing the
spark. Spend time with supportive
friends, go running, swimming or
cycling (anything really, as long as you
can feel the burn) or head out for a
day's exploring.

Try something different:
listen, focus, notice, feel, stay present.
It's harder than it sounds to simply
acknowledge rather than engage with
that push-forwards impulse of yours,
but it will do you good to sink into
the soft place underneath it
all for a little while.

You hate feeling ignored,
disappointed or unacknowledged,
but you must rise above it and forgive
mistakes that have been made.
Forgiving doesn't mean forgetting but
moving on is the only real option now
if you are to continue.

Time to bite the bullet and
ask the right question. Your answer
will lie right in front of you the minute
you are brave enough to ask.

You may feel that some of your
best work comes out of spur-of-the-
moment decisions, but the choice to
aim for a big change is best not made
so impulsively. Sleep on it.

Remember that your ram-headed Aries tendency to bludgeon your way straight to the point doesn't always sit easily with more sensitive souls. Suspend judgement and, if you must have your say, consider all likely outcomes first.

Reset your impulse to charge straight ahead towards what you think looks like the 'correct' solution as though you are aiming straight down a tunnel. Rarely are things this simply resolved. If you can bear to bide your time, wait to see what the universe offers up in due course.

Your adventurous spirit is
strong Aries, and it might be that
you are looking for a new challenge
or exploration right now.
Excitement lies ahead.

Do not allow your focus on future plans to prevent you doing the right thing today. Your impulse is always to charge forwards, like the ram you are, but it is vital that you remain present and focused, retain integrity in all you do.

There are so many people depending on you, you may feel either overwhelmed or spurred on by the adrenaline of it all. It is important to focus on the now, on what you are doing and what you need to do next, rather than letting other people's expectations knock you off-course.

Allow yourself some much needed
downtime today, doing something
you truly love away from work and
home responsibilities. Even one or
two hours will make all the difference,
and you will return refreshed
and recharged.

Prioritize connection and communication Aries, rather than keeping yourself to yourself right now.

Comparing notes and ways of working, and exchanging information, will be a better use of your time right now than lowering your horns and pushing aggressively forwards. You do not have to set yourself on a single track in order to achieve an outcome.

Learning to relax, sweep away negativity, switch off the pressure and quiet the constant hum and buzz of brain-chatter is vital in maintaining your mental and emotional health. Adopt some focused time for yourself, every day, to do just this.

Worrying is counterproductive:
if you can fix something you will,
and if you can't then you need to work
from a more productive angle that will
allow you to reframe the problem.
Endless frustration will result if you
remain distracted by difficulties.
Let them go.

Making a clear plan is your best course of action right now. It is important to figure out what you want for yourself and then pursue it as single-mindedly as you can. Do not allow all the fuss and noise around you to draw your attention away from this important issue.

If it seems that you are not getting through to someone, it might be that they have already made up their minds. You understand stubbornness, don't you Aries? Stop banging your head against a brick wall, and either find a way around them or leave it for now.

Hard-headed and strong-willed, once you make up your mind your opinion is often set – it takes a lot to alter it. But perhaps there is someone or something you were wrong about, or some information you didn't hold before. Soften your heart and head; be prepared to make a change.

Enough is enough Aries; you need to make best use of your energy and trying to bludgeon your way through a seemingly-unbreakable wall might not be the best task to spend time on. This one isn't your problem.

If things are feeling more
difficult than fun with a certain
person, it might be time for a
friendship audit Aries. Not everything
lasts forever, if it's more work than
reward it might be time to honestly
answer the question: is it worth it?

Follow your instincts Aries,
don't allow your thinking logic to
override them or talk you out of what
you know to be true.

Your impulse to rush in headlong
and headstrong will be your enemy on
this one; resist it, lest it leads you
around in a self-defeating circle.

You will need good planning to see this through. Spend some time making sure everything is properly in order before you start, so you can move forwards smoothly.

Shifting your plans and goals around is essential when spring-cleaning your life. Tying up any loose ends, checking in on unsolved problems and making sure everything (and everyone) is up-to-date are all important parts of the process.

Your focused and ram-like persistence takes patience, but really reaps the rewards. Stick with it Aries.

Indecision has a role to play, but
it can be a frustrating process for you
as well as others. Perhaps you are
procrastinating, or trying to tackle
something too difficult? Set it aside for
a while and do something else.

Actually doing something is much more worthwhile and effective than simply thinking about doing something. It might be that you are not sure which way to go because you are afraid, or because you don't have enough information to make a decision. Either way, figure out how to get what you need to make up your mind, and get on with it.

With all that fire flickering through your veins, impatience is a familiar sensation for you Aries. It's particularly easy to feel irritated with indecisive or flighty friends – take some time away from them if this is starting to happen.

All relationships have phases
and your feeling for friends and lovers
will inevitably alter as you (and they)
change and grow. Be honest with
yourself when this is happening and
give yourself (and them) a break.

Don't resist the advice that
people who love you are offering –
it isn't a sign of strength, but just your
ram-stubbornness getting in the way.
A good solution is a good solution; it
doesn't matter that you didn't come
up with it all by yourself.

Your instincts are firing on all cylinders right now Aries – do not second-guess them.

Travel into your own mind while thinking through this issue Aries – there are pockets of memory and learning there that will be useful reference. You have it within you already to solve this one.

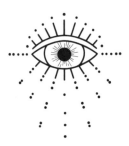

You've nothing to lose by setting pride aside for a short while and asking for help, Aries. Think of it this way: it's not that you can't do it by yourself, but if there is a more efficient, quicker way through that someone else can direct you to, surely, you'd be a fool not to access that experience?

As long as you are sure you're talking to the right people, sharing your ideas is completely worthwhile Aries. But take care when choosing your audience; if they are already committed to a set line of thought, you're wasting your efforts.

Normally so sure-footed Aries,
you might find yourself a little less so
of late. Remain flexible and adaptable,
and it will come right with a little time.
But stay away from tricky terrain
in the meantime if you can.

Keep it light Aries; you will find
that more productive energy comes
your way when you are actively
engaged in a give-and-take exchange.
Find the places for laughter and fun,
and your sparkiness will ignite
plenty of opportunities.

Negativity resonates Aries,
don't put something out there that
you don't want to reverberate and
maybe even make its way back to you.
Adopt a gentle and circumspect
approach and avoid harsh judgements
and sharp words wherever possible.

Emotional confusion is par for
the course with you right now Aries;
there are just too many contradictions
flying about. Pull back from choosing
a particular direction for the moment.

Other people's decisions are not yours to make. The most you can offer is advice and your faith and trust in them to make the right choice for themselves. Their actions are not your responsibility.

Time to think more about other people Aries, and worry less about yourself. Of course, your decisions must still be about you, that's how it works. But less focus on all the little things you think you want and more focus on the greater good is the answer right now.

Share what you have Aries, and
don't give too much thought to 'saving
for best' and 'squirrelling away just in
case' at the moment. Now is not the
time for selfishness.

Giving freely of your time is all that's required now Aries – it might not be that easy, but it will mean a lot.

If you're not quite in the mood for
pushing forwards, listen to yourself
Aries. There is plenty still to be done
without launching off in a
new direction.

Feeling uncertain is not a good launchpad for decisive action Aries. Spend some time instead ensuring you have the full picture and all the facts you need.

Patience is more important than taking a risk this time Aries. Wait a while, let the flames die down, take your time and soon everything will seem clearer.

If you are struggling with particular issues right now Aries, ask (and accept) some advice from those you trust. A different perspective and fresh approach may reveal the angle you need to be working from to get through this.

Take the initiative Aries,
particularly if this is something you
have been wondering about tackling
for a while now. Even if it seems
difficult, take the first few steps, make
that suggestion, hold the door open
and see what happens.

Following your instinct to care
for others can leave you without
enough resources to care for yourself
Aries. Don't drain yourself to
support someone else.

When others can't see the wood
for the trees, as it were, your ability to
point them in the right direction is an
invaluable skill. Help set them on their
path Aries; everyone will benefit from
you assuming this responsibility
and you will feel good about
your contribution.

Holding space for a friend or loved one is a demonstration of how much you care for them. Offer your time, love, support and advice, but then leave them to it. This next step they must take alone.

Drop the weight of your head and give your thinking brain a rest for a little while Aries. There are times when logic rules, and times you have to leave it to one side. This is not a problem that logic alone can solve.

Take control of the situation
if others seem to be floundering –
spinning in circles will not achieve
anything. Convince others to set their
own whims and desires aside for the
time being and focus on what is
best for the team.

Taking care of yourself and your own issues will be a more productive use of your time than casting around for understanding or sympathy from others. It's crucial that you allocate your time wisely right now Aries; there is only just enough of it to cover everything you need to get done.

Set thinking, analyzing and trying
to get this decision right to one side
for now Aries. Embrace the airiness
of your zodiac sign, loosen up and let
the energies of the day move you
along with them, whichever direction
they are travelling.

Pastures new are calling, and the determined ram in you wants to push through the gate and find out what all the fuss is about. Challenging yourself right now will give you a whole new space to shine in and will grow your potential in exciting directions. Positivity all the way – make it happen Aries.

When things seem unclear and uncertain, avoid making very particular decisions if you possibly can. Wait it out and the fog will melt away soon.

Courage is strong with you Aries,
and now is the time to make the most
of it. Accept whatever opportunities
and challenges are coming your
way and tackle them head-on with
your trademark determination and
resourcefulness.

If the pressures are building up,
lose yourself in your favourite films,
books or music for a while to escape.
Allow yourself time to enjoy the
resonance and connection of shared
ideas and beauty, channelling from
giver to receiver. Soak it up.

Taking a break from the world
is essential if you are to rest and
replenish your energy stores properly
Aries. Let yourself sit outside looking
in for a while, and bathe in the calm.

Connecting with relatives and friends is important right now Aries, even more than usual. Check in to see what's happening with everyone and to reaffirm your place within these groups.

With lots of clean, clear energy coming your way, make sure you are primed and ready to take advantage of it. Sweeping through some of the more mundane, everyday tasks that show up on your list right now will mean you are all set to make the most of the surge when it arrives.

A strong leader might be just what the situation requires Aries – are you up to the task? Of course you are. Taking this kind of responsibility might not be your preferred mode, but your talent-bank contains everything you need to make a success of it, and others are relying on you. Time to step up.

Solving problems (and making sure you get the acknowledgement for it) is one of your favourite challenges. Something particularly juicy is on its way. Set your ego and your need to be noticed aside for this one.

Nuance is not your thing Aries,
and you know how frustrating you
find it when others try to pin you
down to the detail. The bold features
and the bigger picture are where
you shine – be honest about this
with yourself and with others.

Surround yourself with good energy
and good people Aries – life is too
short to waste on anything less.

When there is chaos in your
close circle, disentangling can feel
difficult. When everything feels
inefficient and focus is hard to achieve,
it might be that you need to step up
and take control Aries.

Helping others see the benefit in putting their own personal goals aside for the good of the group might be what's required here Aries. Kick your leadership instincts into high gear and illuminate the way for others by setting a shining example. Selflessness and big-picture thinking is required.

As the first of the twelve zodiac signs, you are a trailblazer and a leader, a pioneer who stands forwards rather than shrinking back. Embrace these traits and celebrate them in yourself. Your energetic fire sparks something in everyone you meet.

A cardinal sign, your willpower and self-belief are second to none Aries. You know where you're going and what you're going to do next. If you find yourself unusually confused, or even uncertain, know that this is likely much more about circumstances than it is about you. It will pass.

Your energy and incredible willpower can usually push you forwards and provide the drive required to get things done. You love to be first and you pride yourself on being an original. Stay with these positives in times of stress or unusual pressure. Do not allow a tendency to self-centredness or jealousy to take over.

The energy of your sign is all fire and tenacity Aries; there's a lot of power and push there to take advantage of when you need it. Room to spread out and charge about a bit is important; don't let yourself be forced into too tight a corner.

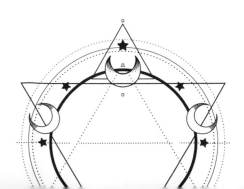

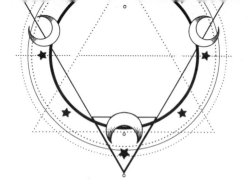

Visualize the life you wish for
yourself Aries – the scaffolding you
put in position now will hold you in
place for the next little while, so be
sure it is shaped as you want it.

Your determined approach can inevitably lead you into willfulness and even stubbornness on occasion. This is something to guard against. Try to work around the people and situations who bring out your worst tendencies; they limit your growth and diminish your potential.

You love a challenge Aries, but
it is important not to overdo it.
Constant pressure will lead you into a
bossy, domineering frame of mind,
which might alienate the very people
you will need to rely on to
get this work done.

Sheer force of will can sometimes provide enough power to get you where you want to go Aries... but that doesn't mean it's always the best, or most elegant, solution.

Self-belief and the willingness
to stand up on behalf of others are
positives Aries; a prideful approach
and recklessness are not. Beware
the shadowy underbelly tendencies
of your sign, and resist impulsivity
and arrogance.

You are the first fire sign in
the zodiac Aries, the first spark
that powers all others that follow.
Pioneering and trailblazing, your
natural talents surge forth and are sure
to get you noticed. Stay on-brand.

With Mars as your ruling planet,
it should be no surprise that
combative energy is woven so
intrinsically into your character Aries.
Guard against hot-headedness that
might engage you in battle too often
though; save it for when it really
matters rather than allowing
confrontation and argumentativeness
to become your fallback position.

Full of confidence, energy and a supreme lust for life, many others look up to you and wonder how you manage to do it all Aries. Well, the truthful answer is probably that you don't mind reverting to selfishness if you feel the situation demands it. Be mindful that this tendency doesn't have a detrimental effect on those closest to you.

You may find yourself in the middle of a surprising conflict Aries. Flex those mediation skills of yours and resolution will be swiftly achieved.

Some coincidences are just too juicy not to take notice of. Grasp them with both hands Aries, and relish the resonance.

A storm cloud might be hovering at the moment Aries, but as long as you help everyone stay focused and cheerful it will pass.

Positive feedback will work
wonders Aries, as will taking the time
to really understand what makes
certain people tick.

Social or networking opportunities that demand your attention may hold promise and potential. Keep your goals in mind during all interactions right now.

Strive for harmony Aries,
especially if you are working with a
partner or colleague at the moment.
A little compromise might be required,
but it's a small price to pay for a
lack of conflict.

Delegate responsibilities according to different talents. It might seem obvious, but now is not the time for stretching to expand skill-sets – everyone needs to work to their existing strengths at the moment.

Collaborations and teamwork
will really pay off Aries; keep your
support team strong around you and
help everyone pull together towards
your common goal.

There's strength in numbers, certainly, but being part of a tribe will only work for you if you really feel you have a place in the group. If that sense of belonging or acceptance is missing, maybe it's time to rethink your affiliations. If everything feels right, stick with it!

As you make more positive progress than perhaps you had expected, the seeds for strong new ventures will be planted.

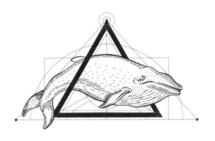

Working together towards a
shared goal will be rewarding and
productive Aries. It is important that
you both acknowledge each other's
effort and input.

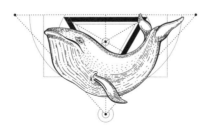

Sometimes, the frustration of feeling that you have fallen behind can be countered by the chance to revisit and revise an issue you hadn't noticed earlier. Embrace the possibilities rather than obsessing over who might be to blame.

Revenge is not the answer Aries;
focus on a cleaner, lighter approach as
you move towards the future instead.

Allow your emotions and intuition
a seat at your decision-making table
Aries. Tune inwards to access an
extra level of wisdom.

Make use of your ram-like determination to explore more of what makes you happy right now Aries, no matter what anyone else thinks you should be doing.

Play is as important as rest when it comes to replenishing your creative juices and allowing yourself some time to unwind. Commit to giving yourself what you need.

Deepening bonds will offer
new possibilities Aries. Whether
these rewards are fated, or achieved
through your own hard work, be sure
to position yourself to take best
advantage of them.

If affirmations and zingy
coincidences are flowing, take
notice Aries. The universe may well be
firing out encouragements, urging
you to continue.

Ease off on the pace Aries;
stubbornly determined as you are,
even you need to relax the pressure on
yourself now and again. Forcing
productivity will simply burn you out.
Let your inner flow rule for the time
being and take advantage of a
more tuned-in vibe.

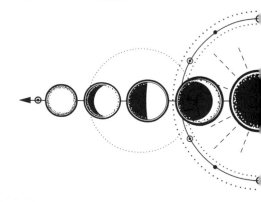

Release thoughts of blame
and feelings of anger Aries; you
are where you are now and simply
need to traverse the ground that
lies in front of you.

Don't ignore your instincts Aries –
there are plenty of options arising, but
not all without potential problems and
pitfalls. Making the right choice will be
about more than simple logic.

Mars, your guardian planet,
blesses you with unsurpassed
determination and vigour; you are
a powerful one Aries. Be sure to
use your strengths to the best of
your abilities – you must focus
on your priorities.

Creativity takes many forms
Aries, whether you are a problem
solver, a free-thinker or a dab hand
with the acrylics or charcoals.
Whatever your outlet and particular
skill, make some time to flex it a little
more than usual. It will do you good.

Free your mind from the relentless obligation-and-delivery wheel, for a little while at least Aries. Commit to filling your own space with your own self, relax and allow everything to realign.

Beware of assurances that
sound too good to be true Aries –
don't allow your intentions to be
derailed by empty promises.

Do not devote your precious
time and attention to situations,
interactions and conversations you
already know to be heading nowhere.
Your self-esteem should be strong
enough that you know to step
decisively away from the
emotional quicksand and
carry on your way.

Do not waste your energy on
worrying about those issues currently
out of your control. Find the smaller
things where you can make the
difference you want to see.

Unexpected developments may seem to hurl a spanner into the works. This might be just one of those times you have to push back against your instincts to be stubborn and loosen up. Giving in to a more flexible flow will bring unexpected positives Aries.

Keep moving Aries, don't allow fuss or temper or tantrums (whether yours or someone else's) to fix you in one place. Your productivity demands that you keep up the momentum.

You might not feel like
sharing your time and space at
the moment Aries, but that doesn't
mean you don't have some great
energy flowing through. You are
perfectly entitled to enjoy it
all by yourself.

Emotional see-sawing is just part of your reality Aries; don't allow it to dampen your enthusiasm or puncture your dream-balloon. Give yourself the time and space you need to recover and carry on strongly.

Don't give up on that long-term
vision Aries, especially not because
of a few pesky feelings. It's very likely
you will wake up tomorrow and
see things differently anyway.
Stick to your plans.

A difference in outlook or values doesn't have to mean a falling out... but sometimes it does. You might not be in a mood to set yourself aside for the sake of social ease right now Aries, and that's just fine.

Use your sharp wit to help
someone who's not quite as quick off
the blocks as you Aries. Just be sure
you're not committing to more than
you can actually deliver.

New people will bring a
fresh perspective. Make the most
of social opportunities when they
present themselves.

Staying open-minded
and clear-headed right now will
mean resolutions quickly follow.
Share the load, if you can,
with someone who also
shares your interests.

Flex your talents when the chance arises Aries – you've plenty to be proud of. Just be mindful not to hog the limelight to avoid unhelpful envy arising in others – allow everyone their opportunity to shine.

Self-care is vital. All that plate-spinning keeps you well and truly focused on the tasks at hand, but you must be sure to set aside some time to recharge as well.

Your quick thinking will give you
a strong advantage Aries.
Make the most of it.

Interacting with those whose company you enjoy is a significant pleasure Aries. If good news and positive opportunities are coming your way at the moment, share them.

Having fun and reaching towards your goals need not be mutually exclusive Aries. Finding a way to combine business and pleasure will enrich both aspects.

It's important to maintain some time for yourself Aries. Build it in, it's all part of a comprehensive maintenance plan.

Solve old problems using fresh insight Aries. New information will come to light and it will make everything look different.

Emotional rejuvenation
requires time and space Aries.
You would be well advised to skip
quickly past anything that seems too
energetic or demanding right now.

Keep your eyes open for someone working away in the background, someone without whom all these good things would not be possible. There is no sense of entitlement or expectation of gratitude... but that doesn't mean that you shouldn't offer it.

Communication and creativity are high on your let's-do-it list right now Aries, and with good reason. Speaking from the heart means that connections will flow, and what comes back to you will be refreshing, revitalizing and pleasingly positive.

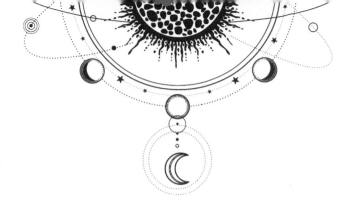

Rising to a challenge is a great feeling Aries; you should be excited about this one and proud of all that you have already achieved.

Disconnecting from obligations
will allow you the freedom to express
and embrace your own needs Aries.

Now is a great time to connect more closely with those who can help you on the way to achieving your goals.

Courageous, driven and generous, you are also a whole lot of fun to be around, especially for others who love a thrill as much as you do. Keep that temper in check and pull back on your tendency to stubborn impulsiveness, and all will go smoothly.

You are a fire sign Aries, and
that makes you a courageous and
dedicated leader. You wear your heart
on your sleeve and that direct
approach endears you to many. But if
detail is required, you should probably
delegate the small-print reading to
someone a little better suited to it.

Focus on harmony and cooperation. Making this work for everyone is the surest way to win.

Forgiveness and release are vital
if you are to lay down the heavy load
you have been carrying and free
yourself Aries. Hope is a beautiful
thing and your future glows with it.

Surprised by an unexpected recent challenge Aries? Your best move would be to sidestep this one and continue your focus on those goals that have been motivating you so strongly.

Remain noncommittal in the
face of a strange or slightly awkward
request Aries. Make your excuses
and absent yourself as
smoothly as possible.

It's not possible or necessary to be best friends with everyone Aries. Just rub along as best you can and treat each other with respect. Appreciate what others bring rather than resenting their shortcomings (as you see them).

Honour your own need to escape from the whirlwind for a while and spend some time by yourself Aries. Everything will seem all the brighter for it.

Avoid chaos as far as you are
able Aries. With so much going on,
there is little extra attention to spare.
What's more, you will start to miss
vital information if your focus
becomes too scattered.
Stay centred.

If confusion relating to a particular situation or relationship still has you scratching your head, make the decision to stick to what you know for now and keep your mind on the tasks in hand.

Interacting and connecting will deliver pleasant results Aries. Hold onto the fun bits and let the rest go – you will enjoy yourself much more that way.

Don't rely on luck to fill the coffers and secure your future Aries – your own creativity will show you the way if you trust, nourish and allow.

Thinking up a neat little
sideline won't be difficult for you
Aries, especially if you follow a
particular creative passion.

If indecision is rife in those around you right now, find a way to make your own call about the parts you can influence, so at least you can get on with something. In the meantime, hold your patience with those who take a little longer to come to their own conclusions Aries.

Bump your own fortunes to the next level Aries, rather than waiting for a return on an investment that might be out of your control at the moment. There is plenty you can do for yourself in the meantime. The rest will come in due course.

Being forced into a routine can bring out your stubborn ram streak Aries – you just don't like it. But it's important to stay the course this time and see what lies at the end of this process: do your time and try not to dwell on it too much.

Setting out hopes for your future should bring joy and hopefulness, rather than conflict and confrontation. If it feels like things are turning in the wrong direction, shelve your forward-planning for the time being and come back to it later.

Step out from the shadows
and show your true colours Aries.
More brightness, lightness and
visibility will go a long way to alerting
others to your presence. A little more
attention might prove to be super-
productive right now.

Remain focused and practical
Aries. This might not be quite what
you always dreamed of, but you
should be reassured that it is a solid
sequence of stepping-stones on
the way there.

Boredom might be implicit right now Aries, but you need to see this through. Going through the motions is fine, as long as you don't make any mistakes. You can dip into your rich interior life to keep yourself amused.

Don't force an answer until you are sure of what you want to say; don't be rushed by other people's urgency.

Sitting on the fence is a delicate balancing act – you need to keep your wits about you.

First published in Great Britain in 2021 by
Greenfinch
An imprint of Quercus Editions Ltd
Carmelite House
50 Victoria Embankment
London EC4Y 0DZ

An Hachette UK company

A CIP catalogue record for this book is available
from the British Library

HB ISBN 978-1-52941-229-1

Every effort has been made to contact copyright holders.
However, the publishers will be glad to rectify in future editions any
inadvertent omissions brought to their attention.

Quercus Editions Ltd hereby exclude all liability to the extent
permitted by law for any errors or omissions in this book and for any loss,
damage or expense (whether direct or indirect) suffered by a third party
relying on any information contained in this book.

10 9 8 7 6 5 4 3 2 1

Designed by Ginny Zeal
Cover design by Andrew Smith
Text by Susan Kelly
All images from Shutterstock.com

Printed and bound in China

MIX
Paper from
responsible sources
FSC® C016973

Papers used by Greenfinch are from well-managed forests
and other responsible sources.